Thank You, God, for Making Me

A Child's Story on Creationism

Diana Gilmer Echols

© 2008 Illustrations by Ron Wheeler.

Pleasant Word (a division of WinePress Publishing, PO Box 428, Enumclaw, WA 98022) functions only as book publisher. As such, the ultimate design, content, editorial accuracy, and views expressed or implied in this work are those of the author.

ISBN 13: 978-1-4141-1012-7
ISBN 10: 1-4141-1012-X
Library of Congress Catalog Card Number: 2007903190

Once upon a time, there was a little boy named Elijah. Elijah asked so many questions that his family always wondered where they came from.

One day Elijah said, "Dad, Mom, how did you get here? How did I get here? Where did the earth come from?" And he went on and on.

At first Elijah's mom and dad thought the questions were funny, but they knew they had to answer. So Dad said, "God created me, Mommy, you, and the earth."

"Wow!" said Elijah. "We were created by God? God did all of this? How?" he asked.

Elijah's parents started to tell him the story. They said God created the heavens and the earth.

Mom said, "One day God looked around the space we call earth and said, 'There is no shape or life.' The space was dark and gloomy. So God spoke to the darkness and said, 'Let there be light.'"

"All of a sudden the earth had light, and God separated the light from the darkness. God called the light 'daytime' and the darkness 'nighttime.'

"This ended the first day of God's creation."

Genesis 1:3–5

Elijah got so excited. "Wow, Mom! God created light and darkness. That is cool. All God did was say it and it happened? Wow, Mom, wow!"

Elijah's mother laughed and said, "Elijah, are you going to let us finish?"

Elijah said, "Yeah, Mom, please finish. God sounds so cool. What else did He do?"

"The next day," said Dad, "God looked at all the water that covered everything and said, 'Let the water be separated.' And the water was separated. God called the space high above the water the 'heavens.'"

"Oh, Dad, God is awesome," said Elijah. "He just told the water to separate and it did. All that water? Oh, God is awesome."

"Yes, God is awesome," said Dad, "and you know what? Separating the water from the heavens ended the second day."

Genesis 1:6–8

"But, Dad," said Elijah, "where did the earth come from? Where is the land that we live on?"

"That happened on the next day."

"Oh," said Elijah. "Please finish telling me."

"On the third day," said Dad, "God told the waters to come together so that dry land could exist. Once God spoke it, the waters joined together, and dry land appeared."

"Guess what?" Elijah's mom said. "The dry land is what God called 'earth,' and we live on the earth. But God was not finished with the earth yet."

"What did He have left to do?" asked Elijah.

"God wanted to make sure that the earth had something on it," said Mom.

"Something like what?" asked Elijah.

"God told the earth to make fruit, grass, and trees—and the earth did!"

"No way, Mom. Are you fibbing? God did not tell the earth to make grass."

"Yes, He did, Elijah. Would I lie to you?" said Mom.

"No, but—oh, man, Mom, God is so cool. God is awesome!"

"Yes, God is awesome," said Mom. "And that is how God ended the third day."

Genesis 1:9–12

Dad continued. "On the fourth day—"

"Dad, hold up. What about people? How did we get here?" asked Elijah.

"Elijah, that part of the story is coming. You will have to wait to see how God made people."

"OK, I just thought people would have been here by now."

Elijah's dad laughed and said, "That part is coming. Just be patient, son. Now, on the fourth day, God made the moon, sun, and stars."

"Oh, man!" said Elijah. "God made the sun, moon, and stars? How did He do that? Wait! Let me guess! God spoke it and it was."

"You are so smart, Elijah," said Dad. "Yes, that is what happened. God created the sun to make the day and the moon and the stars to make the night."

"Was God finished with the fourth day?" Elijah asked.

"Yes," said Mom.

"Well, what about the fifth day?" asked Elijah.

"We are getting there," Mom and Dad said together.

Genesis 1:14–16

"Guess what God created next, Elijah,"
said Dad.

"He created people. Yeah!"

"Not yet," Dad said. "He created animals
that live in the air and in the water."

"Wow, Dad, I forgot about animals. It
sounds like God created everything."

"God did create everything, Elijah, He did. Then God told the birds of the air and the creatures of the sea to make a lot of themselves."

"No wonder there are so many birds," said Elijah. "God told them to make a lot. Is that why there are a lot of people? Did God tell people to make a lot?"

Elijah's parents laughed and said, "Yes, we are getting to that part of the story."

Genesis 1:20–23

"On the last day of God's creation, guess what He made," said Mom.

Elijah yelled, "He made people!"

"Yes, Elijah. God made a man called Adam, then a woman called Eve on the last day."

"I bet you I know how He did it, Mom," said Elijah.

"How did He do it, Elijah?"

"God said, 'Let there be people,' and people appeared like everything else."

"Good try, Elijah, but God made Adam and Eve in a very special way that is different from how God created everything else."

"Really, Mom? How did God do it?"

"Well, before God created people, He first made animals for the land."

"Like dogs, bugs, and cows, Mom?"

"Yes, like dogs, bugs, and cows."

"Ooh, and dinosaurs and bears?"

"Yes, Elijah, you get the idea."

"OK, Mom, what about people?"

"Remember I told you that God created Adam and Eve differently from everything else?"

"Yes," said Elijah.

"God said to Himself, 'Let's make man like Us and let man rule everything that has been created.'"

"What did He mean by 'like Us'?" asked Elijah.

~

Genesis 1:24–26

"Well, God wanted to make people so that they could live on the earth and have a relationship with God," said Mom. "God wanted to be able to talk to them, and God wanted them to have the ability to choose right from wrong and love from hate. To do this, God had to make a man to get things started. God formed Adam from the dust and put life into Adam by blowing into his nose, and Adam became a living man."

"Mom! Mom! God breathed Himself into Adam? So does that mean that God was in Adam?"

"Yes, it does."

"Do I have God in me?" asked Elijah.

"We all have God in us," said Mom.

"Wow! God must have wanted man to be special. Did God make Eve the same way?"

"No, son. Eve was also made differently."

"How, Dad? How did God make Eve?"

Genesis 2:7

"Son," Dad said, "would you believe God put Adam to sleep and took a bone from Adam and made Eve for him? And that is how God created the world and made men and women. He told Adam and Eve to make a lot of themselves, and they did. They had children who had children. Eventually your grandparents were born, and they had Mommy and me, and we had you."

"Wow! Wow!" said Elijah. "We all come from Adam and Eve. God is amazing! He made everything."

Genesis 2:21–22

Elijah just smiled and said "Thank You, God, for making me and Mom and Dad. Thank You, God, for everything!"

Pleasant Word

To order additional copies of this title call:
1-877-421-READ (7323)
or please visit our Web site at
www.pleasantwordbooks.com

If you enjoyed this quality custom-published book,
drop by our Web site for more books and information.

www.winepressgroup.com
"Your partner in custom publishing."

Printed in the United States
140365LV00003B